WORKING SMART: YOUR GUIDE TO BUILDING A PROFITABLE BUSINESS IN THE PRESENT ECONOMY

Nicholas Smith

Table of contents

Chapter 1

Setting yourself up for success in the present economy and how not to struggle with burnout.

The present economy is bad and may go worse with the recession and inflation, it's simply ridiculous. We simply have to discover methods to survive and prosper both as people and company entrepreneurs. A terrible economy might fully take up your small firm if you're not strategic enough. Let's start with how this economy affects business.

How Does a Bad Economy Affect Business?

A terrible economy may affect a firm in a variety of ways. Adjustments to interest rates might impair a business's capacity to borrow critical capital. People preserving their money during a moment of economic uncertainty might imply they are spending less and so the firm has fewer consumers. Some industries may come to a relative stop if the market falls significantly.

But what you don't realize is the more terrible the economy, the larger the prospects but only for those who are strong, well-prepared, and tenacious. Many individuals are obsessed with national or even global economic dread and gloom. Many wait for a miracle remedy, only to learn it will never happen.

When circumstances get bad for your small company, it is crucial at that moment, more than ever, to have a cool head. Sometimes, there is a simple remedy that may assist you to keep the company going that you wouldn't have recognized if you were too anxious or weighed down by little details. Being aware of the broad picture and making sure you as the number one employee are functioning effectively are the number one priority during a moment of adversity. Which brings us to:

9 core things you need to do that'll set you up for success

1. *Try to obtain greater control of your cash flow:*
   If you want to endure this difficult economic scenario, you must maintain an eagle watch on your cash flow. Up your game. Know your figures on daily basis. Know your ROI per transaction. Are you earning profits or losses? Just make sure you keep your head above the water all the while throughout this duration.

2. *Avoid needless expenses*:

You must be aware of your company spending. Yes, now is the moment to reduce unnecessary bonuses, useless vacations, unanticipated incentives, and other stuff that has no direct influence on your company's success.

3. *Be more strategic by raising your budget and costs concerning marketing and advertising:*
   This is not the greatest moment to cut down on your marketing budget, rather pick a marketing approach that has the potential to expand your share of the market, and invest aggressively in the plan.

4. *Run your company on a pay-as-you-go:*
   Limit your costs to sales earned during this period. This is not the finest moment to get into debt for the sake of your company; rather you cut

your coat according to your cloth. Put aggressive efforts towards growing sales to compensate for your overheads and company costs.

5. *Let the survival of your company be your ultimate goal:*
   Your ultimate approach should be how to make your firm relevant in the marketplace at this point among the competition. Think out of the box. Create a powerful team that will assist design the plan to navigate through the storm. Be cognizant of all the business and market indications for and against the survival of your firm and know how to operate around them.

6. *Take care of your existing customers:*
   Your consumers are your company's biggest assets. Sourcing new consumers will cost you

more energy and resources in comparison to sustaining your present ones. Without your clients, your company will cease to exist. Existing clients are the most vital factor in surviving a challenging time. Take care of them and they will soon become the faithful ones sharing the gospel of your company so generating recommendations for you.

7. *Motivate your workers* (if you have people working for you)
   In a moment like this, most employees would be in a state of fear, particularly now that there are reports that certain banks and MNCs are laying off people. Treat your personnel with dignity despite the terrible economic realities. This may seem contradictory, but it will work to your benefit. With this, your personnel will make your company theirs since they

will come to know you're providing them a fantastic favor and they need to return by making sure the business works.

8. *Keep consulting*:
   In a circumstance like this, one definite method not to become extinct is to keep studying and consulting. Keep talking to specialists and peers in your business. Share expertise and discuss with them. There is synergy in dealing with other individuals, it gives you informed knowledge in the industry.

9. *Never tamper with quality*:
   Do not be frustrated into believing that by interfering with the quality of your goods or services, your firm will be able to survive. No, it will not take long before your clients start to recognize it, and subsequently, choose to

patronize rivals with superior deals. You may increase your cost depending on economic realities to secure your existence, definitely not by interfering with the quality you give. Easier said than done right? You just have to take a breather, grab your planner and write down how you can follow through with the above steps and just getting your business back on track. This is your business, take back control.

With all these said, you might feel overwhelmed with everything. Fear of the current state of your small company, keeping a cool head, and just making crucial decisions. Let's talk about:

How not to deal with burnout

This section is paramount. Going through these processes might be tough on you, so this will come in handy.

What is burnout?

Simply described, burnout is a condition of physical, mental, and emotional weariness produced by excessive, severe, or persistent stress. It is often characterized by a lack of energy or motivation and a feeling of pessimism or cynicism, as well as greater mental detachment from one's profession. Unlike with typical exhaustion, persons suffering burnout may feel overwhelmed or incapable of dealing with stress or managing tasks. Burnout may also lead to problems with concentration and diminished work effectiveness. Though often tied to one's profession, issues such as child care, work-life balance, societal pressure, and social media, may also worsen feelings of stress and anxiety and contribute to burnout.

Preventing and Managing Burnout

The good news is that burnout is preventable. Whether you're suffering burnout now or think you're headed down that road, here are some techniques to safeguard your mental health.

1. Practice Healthy Habits

Taking care of your physical health is one of the finest methods to boost your mental health. In times of intense stress, it's crucial not to let healthy habits slide through the cracks. This entails keeping a nutritious diet, obtaining a good night's sleep, practicing proper hygiene, and exercising frequently. Try to consume healthful meals, while being cautious of your caffeine and alcohol intake. Alcohol is a depressive and may drastically impair your mood, motivation, energy, and sleep, even days later. Meanwhile, coffee is a stimulant that we might become unduly reliant on when we're already burned out. You should also reduce your sugar and refined carb intake, since both may leave you feeling sluggish and low energy. Try to go to bed at the same time each night, aim for at least 7 to 8 hours of sleep. Research reveals that obtaining fewer than 6 hours of sleep might raise your risk of burnout since it can influence your productivity, focus, and motivation. Likewise, regular exercise can enhance your mood, increase your attention, and help you sleep better. Even exercising only 10 to 20 minutes of exercise a day may greatly enhance your overall happiness level and decrease stress.

2. Set borders!

One of the major drivers of burnout is a lack of a healthy, work-life balance. For many, however, it's been difficult to establish a

clear division between the two when working from home.
Without a commute or physically leaving the workplace, it might be easy to become caught up in a job and work longer or later hours. Create a new at-home commute by taking a little stroll around the block and listening to a podcast or music. If you used to read on the metro or train on your way home from work, pick up a book or listen to an audiobook at home after you finish working. Replicating this travel time will help you disengage and more quickly shift to your non-work activities. Do the same in the morning, by sipping a cup of coffee or reading the news before diving immediately into work. It might also be good to designate a distinct portion of your house for work alone. This might be a guest room, workspace, or even simply a corner of your flat. This location should be distinct from where you go to rest, watch TV, or decompress, to avoid the stress of work

from infecting your other activities. Likewise, try to create clearly defined working hours by switching off your computer and shutting off email alerts at a regularly planned time each day.

3. Make time for fun

Oftentimes, we get so wrapped up in our day-to-day chores or caring for others, that we forget to create time purely for pleasure. Engaging in things you like may help you recharge and destress, and return to your job or duties with a more positive attitude. Hobbies may also distract you from regular worries, make you feel more in the present, and eventually increase your job performance. You don't have to carve out a great lot of time for these activities either. Do a 10-minute yoga session, work on a puzzle, read a book for bed, attempt a new dish for supper, or even simply play with your cat for a few minutes. Even merely finding methods to enliven your routine duties will assist, Ask yourself, What offers me joy? Then identify and create organized chances to integrate it throughout your day.

4. Take frequent breaks

When we're feeling burned out, we aren't as productive or creative as we typically would be. Whether you're working from home, homeschooling, caring for children, or experiencing other pressures, it's crucial to take frequent breaks throughout the day to return to your job or obligations with a fresh, rejuvenated perspective. Try setting an alarm, giving yourself reminders, or arranging periodic breaks into your calendar. This might be for lunch, a short snack or coffee, a stroll around the house, or simply for a few minutes of stretching.

5. Practice mindfulness

Practicing mindfulness may decrease stress, help you feel more anchored in the present, and help you remain in touch with your emotions. For other individuals, mindfulness may involve breathing exercises like this body scan or beginning a gratitude diary. Spending time being aware of your surroundings is a terrific approach to be present and optimistic in times of increased stress. A fantastic method to develop mindfulness is to engage as many of your senses as possible in one activity. For example, wash dishes using aromatic dish soap, be mindful of the feeling of the bubbles, and hear the squeak of the gloves. For others, it may entail walking outdoors and watching the environment around you, paying attention to the sounds, scents, and views of the outdoors. Studies have proven that physically immersing oneself in nature has the power to alleviate stress and anxiety, as well as improve your mood. You might also try concentrating your attention on something that needs active thinking and concentration, like reading a detailed book or going on a bike ride.

6. Take time off

While microbreaks each day may be a terrific method to decrease stress, time apart from your typical routine can be exceptionally refreshing. Use your well-earned paid time off to plan a trip and give yourself something to look forward to. If you can't afford to take a trip right now, even simply giving yourself a mental health day will help your recharge. For some this may mean, taking a day off from work, while for others it may mean merely utilizing a weekend day to sleep, eat properly, and rest Give yourself time to reset and remind yourself that taking the time to recharge makes you more productive and efficient and may minimize your stress and symptoms of burnout

7. Reach out to loved ones

Burnout is typically accompanied by feelings of loneliness, but it's crucial to realize that you're not alone. Many others are coping with similar thoughts right now and it might help to discuss your experiences with supportive loved ones or retain a channel of open communication with your superiors or coworkers. Sharing these sentiments may help you feel less alienated and more positive, as well as find out strategies to better manage your workload.

With everything that has gone on around the globe in the previous year, it's reasonable that you may feel burned out or fatigued. Luckily, these sensations are neither permanent nor inescapable. If you feel like you are dealing with your mental health right now, reach out to your primary care physician so that you can work on a treatment plan.

8. Deal with decision fatigue

Decision weariness arises every day in your life as well. If you have a very decision-heavy day at work, then you arrive home feeling weary. You could want to go to

the gym and exercise, but your brain would prefer to default to the simple decision: sit on the sofa. That's decision weariness.
The same thing is true whether you find it hard to conjure up the motivation to work on your side company at night or to make a nutritious meal for supper.
And although decision fatigue is something that we all suffer from, there are a few ways that you can arrange your life and plan your day to dominate your willpower.

Ways to conquer **Decision Fatigue**

1. Plan daily choices the night before.
There will always be choices that spring up each day that you can't prepare for. That's OK. It's simply part of life.
But for most of us, the choices that exhaust us are the ones that we make over and over again. Wasting valuable willpower on these choices which might be automated or prepared in advance is one reason why

many individuals feel so fatigued at the end of the day.
For example, choices like…
What am I going to wear to work? What should I eat for breakfast? And so forth.
All of those situations above can be determined in 3 minutes or less the night before, which means you won't be spending your willpower on those decisions the following day. Taking time to plan out, simplify, and design recurring everyday decisions will allow you more mental space to make critical choices each day.

2. Do the most essential item first.
This applies to your job and life. What’s the most important thing for you at the moment? Is it getting in shape? Is it building your business? Is it learning to remove tension and relax?
Whatever it is for you, put your best energy into it. If you have to get up 30 minutes earlier, then do that. Start your day by

working on the most important item in your life.

3. Stop making choices. Start making commitments.
I believe advice like, “you only need to decide to do it” is given around too often.
Yes, of course, you need to decide to do the things that are essential to you, but more than that you need to plan them into your life.
We all have things that we say are essential to us.

“I genuinely want to expand my business.”

“I want to get started on my new idea.”
Unfortunately, most of us just hope that we'll have the willpower and determination to make the correct judgments each day.
Rather than expecting that I'll make the appropriate decision each day, I've found far

greater success by scheduling the activities that are essential to me.

For example, my timetable for writing is Tuesday and Friday. My timetable for working out is Monday, Wednesday, and Friday. On any given Tuesday, I don't have to determine if I'm going to write. It's already on the schedule. And I'm not optimistic that I'll have the resolve to work out It's simply what I do on Mondays at 6 pm.
If you sit back and hope that you'll be able to make the proper judgments each day, then you will undoubtedly fall prey to decision fatigue and a lack of willpower.

4. If you have to make excellent judgments later in the day, then eat something beforehand.

Now, if you stuff french fries into your veins every day, then I doubt that you'll have the same effects. But pausing to fuel your brain is a fantastic approach to building willpower.

This is particularly crucial because while it’s excellent to accomplish the most important item first, it’s not always practical to plan your day like that.

When you want to receive better choices from your head, put better nourishment into your body.

5. Simplify.

Whether you are aiming to attain the maximum level of performance or merely want to start eating a healthy diet, the biggest annoyance for most people is the sensation that you need to exercise willpower on an hourly basis.

Find strategies to simplify your life. If something isn't significant to you, delete it. Making judgments on insignificant things, even if you have the leisure to do so, isn't a benign endeavor. It's stealing valuable energy and willpower from the things that count.

Willpower is one area of life where you can most surely enhance your output by minimizing the number of inputs.

Chapter 2

Finding the online business for you and how to make your offline company grow online

Ok so let's say you want to establish an internet company but you don't know what business to do, what will favor you or what you'll be fantastic at.

I'll be offering you a few successful business ideas and how to recognize whether it's genuinely fitted with you, your personality, and your purpose.

Starting an internet company, no matter how tiny you plan to have it may cost time and money.

Do not worry however since once you get the wheels turning on your journey, launching an internet enterprise will be enjoyable and inspiring. Since a wonderful source of revenue, side hustle chances are many as you don't need to be positioned next to a consumer to give the products or services to them.

1. If you see yourself as a creative person, a person who likes design and editing, you can go into one of these
    - T-shirt online store: websites like Shopify have made it easy to start a T-shirt online store and if you think you have a lot of designs in your head and would like to make it a reality, maybe a T-shirt online store is for you. My perspective on this is simply your designs should be distinctive and catchy.

    - Graphics design is not that hard as long as you know the fundamentals. You have to understand the basics and then build from there. If you didn't know, there is a lot of money to be earned in graphic design. A lot of firms require employees with the expertise.

- Video production/content creation if you are extremely excellent at filming anything maybe just maybe video production might be for you.

2. If you're a tech person try checking out these

- You can be a website developer. A lot of business owners, organizations and personal brands need a person with this skill. This is a high-income skill as long as you're good at it, you don't need to aggressively promote yourself. Just show them what you can do and if you don't know how to develop websites but you're interested, you can easily learn it. Every website developer learned it too.

- App development is a pretty profitable ability as well. Companies are searching for app developers to create their apps, Offering app development is a terrific opportunity as you may work on drastically diverse applications daily.

3. If you enjoy being on social media, you may as well earn money, right?

- You may be a social media manager. Many company owners are prepared to outsource this time-intensive activity, therefore it’s a terrific chance for social media junkies.

Bundle together a few attractive services, such as "Startup social media kit" or "Small Business Social Media Starter Kit" that contain everything from social media visuals to analytics reports and the seamless experience will bring you more customers than you think.

- Becoming an influencer
  An influencer is someone with a significant fan base on social media who is considered an expert in a certain subject, such as cosmetics or fitness. These people remain occupied by writing constantly about their life and advertising things that they believe are beneficial to acquire. What is fantastic about this online business concept is that

you may be paid to promote a company to your followers,

- A YouTuber
  There are several categories/niches you can get into on YouTube. Find a topic you're interested in establishing a following and see where that leads you. You may check on YouTube if you want advice from a successful YouTuber. Checking what a YouTuber in your niche already does and learn.

4. Anyone can do it
   - Affiliate marketing
     Affiliate marketing is when a person promotes a product that another merchant offers. Using advertising, social media,

blogging, and more, an affiliate marketer may drive clients to their landing page. When clients click a link to purchase the product they will then be transported to the merchant's shop to buy the product.

- Dropshipping is the simplest approach to start an e-commerce company without needing to acquire any things in advance. Use dropshipping applications to locate thousands of items from suppliers to sell online. Then sell to clients throughout the globe while establishing and marketing your brand, all without having to invest in storage or production expenditures. You don't need to pay for inventory until it's sold to an actual client

5. If you're good at writing, you might check into CV writing, Speechwriting and being a self published author.

6. If you're excellent with languages You can be a foreign language teacher or translator.
There are plenty more concepts out there that I potentially can't address in one book.

Actions you need to take to establish your company

1. Decide Your Business
This is the most critical phase since without it you don't have a company. Check out the above list and determine which one fits you best.

2. Research Your Industry

Get to know what your industry is like. Maybe there is a price structure most of your rivals adopt that will be excellent for you. Or maybe after you find your competition you will determine that your sector is over-saturated and you need to tweak your company concept somewhat to compete.

3. Create Your Brand

With every good company comes a good brand and if you figure this out at the start you may become a more successful online business in the beginning. This involves having a beautiful website, and social media (if your consumers are there), killer logo development, participating in some PR, and some additional outreach and marketing efforts.

4. Begin Getting Customers

The last step to getting started is gaining your first client. Having fantastic consumers behind you implies success for your firm. To identify these consumers you need to learn how to get in front of your audience, put out the proper message to attract customers, and design a price structure that works for the majority of customers to successfully provide them with what they need.

Chapter 3

HOW TO DRIVE GROWTH WITH CUSTOMER SUCCESS

Okay, let's pretend you already have a company. You market your goods and services on your social media channels but you're still not having sales. So you want more eyes on your products/services online?

You need to have a user-friendly website. It may seem difficult but it merely makes sales easier. The reality is, the internet has made it easier to launch a company. With simply a website, you may contact anybody in any place around the globe. Target the appropriate folks with the proper offers, and you would be earning your own money in no time. After constructing your website I'll be talking about how you can obtain traffic, and

how you can attract people to purchase your stuff on your website.
The connection you develop with your current clients might help you break into new areas, or it could freeze your growth.
But customer success may develop even deeper ties and spark huge corporate growth.

Customer success is when you allow your customers to accomplish commercial or personal progress and reach their objectives utilizing your product or service.
It entails adopting a proactive response to customers' concerns and lowering the number of obstacles the consumer has while working with your brand.
When the consumer has a nice experience with your company, this fosters loyalty and advocacy, and generates growth in your company.

Customer success doesn't simply happen by luck; you need to strategize and develop a focused task force to accomplish it.

Let’s dig into additional specifics.

Key Areas in Customer Success That Drive Business Growth

Adoption

Sometimes referred to as onboarding, adoption is the stage when clients grow habituated to your product or service.

You must coach your new client into utilizing your product or service in a manner that gives maximum value and helps them achieve growth.

To achieve this properly, you need to understand your customers’ wants and aspirations and then deliver a commensurate solution.

Retention

Every time a consumer quits using your product, you lose income, which inhibits company development.

Retention entails ensuring that your product continually gives value to your consumer, which keeps them engaged.

You need to review the customers' wants and aspirations from time to time and ensure that your product or service fits their demands.

Successful adoption and retention will achieve two things for your business:

- *Promote growth* – Having maintained your consumer satisfaction to the point of continuing loyal to your business, they're inclined to spend more with your firm. This increases business growth.
- Promote referrals – If your consumer experiences success,

they will likely suggest your items to a friend. This boosts your market share while boosting growth.

Here are two methods that may help you enhance client success.

1. Build a Highly Effective Customer Success Team
   No matter your organization's size, you need a committed staff to develop a proactive connection with your clients, nurturing your business's success.
   Each team member should know their role in creating customer success, both individually and with the team.
   Depending on your business's size, build a clear framework to

support seamless operations within the team.

Here are some responsibilities you may include:

Head of Customer Success – Is responsible for establishing and executing customer success strategies and monitoring the customer success team's development.

Customer Success Analyst - Studies customer data to uncover trends that might assist establishing successful customer success initiatives.

Customer Success Manager - Works directly with customers. Identifies customers' business objectives and predicts how to satisfy them.

You may segment your consumers depending on their requirements and

expectations for your firm. Then, designate people or groups of team members to manage customer success in each section. By doing so, you will boost your team's effectiveness, resulting in greater growth rates.
However, make careful to hire the ideal personnel for your team to nurture client success and support company development.
Customer success team members should display:

- Strategic thinking
- Metacognition and empathy
- Excellent communication skills
- Social skills
- Proactive problem-solving skills

A thorough grasp of customer success and its influence on company growth

With this strategy, the customer team will better understand the customers and interact with them more successfully.

2. Create an Effective Strategy
   To accomplish company development via customer success, you need a comprehensive plan. It should comprise offering continuous and excellent customer care to your clients from the adoption stage till they achieve success and growth utilizing your product or service.
   Your company's goods and services are destined to develop. So will the requirements of your consumers

and the environment around them. Modify your approach to fit these changes.

Although the customer success team is responsible for helping the customers succeed, the team shouldn't operate alone.

- Embrace cross-functionality and establish open communication channels across multiple departments.

- Bake your customer success strategies into everything the firm does. All interactions with clients at every step in your company should be consistent with these tactics. This will make it simpler to achieve customer success and company development.

Quickly execute your customer success plan by investing in the proper tools.

- Use Customer Data as best as you can.

Every time a consumer interacts with your organization, they create important data. Gather this data at numerous places to gain a thorough picture of the customer's journey. Analyzing the data may help you extract practical insights that support company success, such as:

- Areas where you need to improve the customer's experience.

- The product characteristics that your clients enjoy most and least.

- Warning indications of consumers in danger of switching to a rival.

Keep this data in a central area where all teams may access it.
Be sure to retain real-time data on your clients to remain current on their changing requirements and objectives. Having this information readily accessible will help your customer success team to react immediately to these developments.

- Educate Your Customers While Applying SEO Techniques
  With lots of data on how your clients engage with your business or corporation, you may foresee difficulties that are likely to develop. Use this material to solve frequent pain points before they become a bother to your consumers.

- Educate clients on how to address their day-to-day issues utilizing your goods and services.

- Create a knowledge base on your website with a FAQ section, or utilize a content calendar to guarantee you produce information on time.

- Incorporate SEO methods into your article. Marketing with tailored content may help you reach new audiences. It generates organic traffic to your website and enhances growth.

- When educating your consumers, keep it simple no need to overwhelm them with your product or service's technical specifics. Instead, concentrate on the value your product or service will provide to their lives or company.

- Personalization Is Key to Customer Success
  Similar to how customized marketing works, you may customize your customer outreach to boost customer success and accomplish growth.

- Assign team members to all your client segments. The team may then concentrate on the particular wants and objectives of the clients in each category.
  For instance, if you have a new product coming up that will be especially important to a certain consumer, a team member may individually chat to them about it. Likewise, if a client is seeing

development in their company, congratulate them.

NOTE: There's no need to worry if you don't have a team yet.

When it comes to more broad communication formats, such as product portfolios, customize every segment's message.
Speaking directly about what your consumer needs encourages them towards attaining their objectives with your product or service.
Personalization is a big growth factor. It helps your consumers feel appreciated and develops loyalty.

Get Ready To Achieve Business Growth Through Customer Success
Successful company models and marketing executives put customer success at the center of their growth strategy.

When the consumers are delighted, they stay loyal and become devoted ambassadors for the brand. These two variables fuel company development and might expose you to new markets.
Hop on the bandwagon. Make customer success an intrinsic component of your marketing growth strategy and establish a strong team to execute it. Educate your consumers and track their journey to guarantee they obtain optimum value from your goods or services. And be sure to appropriately steer your consumers towards success by being in touch with their specific demands.

Newer marketing methods arise as customers grow more aware of a digital world that responds to their wants. Keep up with the newest trends and forecasts in different sorts of email marketing to remain on the top of your game.

Email Marketing Campaign

Okay, in this section, you're going to come across a lot of new terms so try not to get overwhelmed. Just read it carefully, line by line or just come back.

Email marketing has grown more significant in recent years, and it will only continue to do so in the future. To remain ahead of the curve in 2022 and beyond, make sure you follow the email marketing recommendations below to produce market-leading email marketing campaigns.

1. Create Irresistible Lead Magnets
A fantastic way for boosting sign-ups is to employ an efficient lead magnet. Gone are the days when simply newsletters would fetch you your

target audience' information. In 2022, you have to be inventive in generating email marketing concepts and producing engaging lead magnets for clients to sign up. Apart from newsletters, you may give leads like Ebooks, Swipe files, case studies, etc., which may help you expand your subscriber base.

2. Mobile Optimization

Today, 81% of all emails are opened and read on mobile devices. Mobile optimization is crucial for any email marketing plan in this day and age. You need to ensure that all of your customers have the same great experience when seeing your email regardless of where they check it!

3. Design Your Emails Well

Email users commonly skim through the text and dismiss emails that don't give value or are too complex. This is why it's vital to pay attention to the aesthetic aspect of your email to attract the attention of your receivers. Layout, colors, fonts, and images all add to the branding and professionalism of your emails. Your readers will know your brand if you use colors and a layout that represents its personality. Keeping your emails succinct and sweet and using a good template will make them aesthetically attractive to the receiver.

4. Hyper-Personalize Your Emails

Hyper customization is one of the largest and most current email marketing strategy examples for 2022, and it is here to stay. Hyper-personalization employs artificial intelligence and real-time data to present clients with more relevant information. Consumers demand customized experiences and they tend to flock to businesses that communicate directly to them. While many marketers are aware of this, they aren't tailoring their communications as much as they should be. Email hyper-personalization fast becomes the norm for converting leads into customers and consumers into brand supporters.

5. Measuring Success

Key Performance Indicators (KPIs) are used to assess and monitor the performance of email marketing initiatives. KPIs enable you to assess whether or not you've reached your marketing goals. They'll also start to identify tendencies that you may employ to increase the efficacy of your emails. If you want to maintain your email list, maximize the ROI (Return

On Investment) of your campaigns, you need to monitor a few important metrics periodically. The three KPIs described below might help you assess your email marketing performance.

Open Rates

Increasing open rates may be as easy as personalizing your emails or adopting a brief subject line.

Email Engagement

It's vital to understand your subscribers' habits and schedules so you can reach out to them more effectively. By delivering your emails at optimal times, you may boost user engagement.

Click-Through Rate

Examining email conversations could assist you to find out what sort of material your clients appreciate. Increase your Click-through rate by emphasizing call-to-action buttons.

Email Marketing Strategy Against Spams

Measuring the success of your email marketing enables you to learn from your errors and make your emails more effective. Moreover, dynamic layouts and templates improve engagement and grow more popular as technology develops.

Make sure you have a social media marketing approach

1. What is social media marketing?

Let's begin things off by addressing the big question.

Putting it simply, social media marketing is harnessing social media channels to promote your brand and sell your product or service. Just like you prepare other areas of your marketing strategy, you need to have a plan for your social media marketing.

2. Set objectives that make sense for your company

Social media strategy planning begins with your objectives.

Whether you want to grow a bigger following or a more engaged community, taking the time to outline your social objectives is the first step to accomplishing them.

Either way, your objectives will determine your social media marketing approach and how much time and energy you'll need to spend on your campaigns.

What's important is that you create realistic social media objectives.

Emphasis on "realistic," by the way. We advocate targeting smaller targets that enable you to increase your social activities in a manner that's both feasible and cheap.

Below are some example objectives that companies of all shapes and sizes may pursue.

Increase brand awareness.

This entails getting your name out there. To establish true and enduring brand awareness, avoid just releasing promotional messaging. Instead, concentrate on material that promotes your personality and ideals first.

Generate leads and sales.

Whether online, in-store, or directly via your social accounts, followers don't make purchases by mistake. For example, are you about updating consumers about new items and promos? Are you connecting your product catalog to your social profiles? Are you providing unique bargains for followers?

Grow your brand's audience.

Bringing new followers into the fold requires finding methods to present your brand to those who haven't heard of you before.

Growing your audience also requires uncovering topics around your brand and sector that matter the most. Digging through your social networks is practically hard without monitoring or listening for certain keywords, phrases, or hashtags. Having a pulse on these topics helps you increase your core audience (and reach adjacent groups) much more quickly.

Boost community involvement. Index research reveals that 46% of consumers say businesses that engage their audience are best in class on social, therefore it pays to seek new methods to catch the attention of your present followers. This requires experimenting with the message and content. For example, does your brand support user-generated content and hashtags?
Even something as easy as asking a question might raise your engagement rate. Your consumers may be your finest

cheerleaders, but only if you're offering them something to do.

Drive traffic to your site. Simple enough. Whether via promotional posts or social advertisements, keeping an eye on conversions and URL clicks will help you better evaluate your ROI from social media.
Any combination of these objectives is fair game and may help you better determine which networks to attack, too. When in doubt, keep your social media marketing approach basic rather than cluttering it with too many goals that could distract you. Pick one or two and rally your squad behind them.

3. Take time to study your target audience
Making assumptions is terrible news for marketers.
Only 55% of marketers utilize social analytics to better understand their target audience, making it a big potential for both

executives and practitioners. Much of what you need to know about your audience to affect your social media marketing plan is already accessible. You only need to know where to look.

With the correct technology, marketers can swiftly investigate their audience. No formal market research or data science expertise is required.

Remember: various channels draw different audiences.

Take today's social media demographics, for example. These stats speak directly to which networks your brand should contact and what sorts of content to promote. Here are some critical lessons for your 2022 social media marketing strategy:

Facebook and YouTube are both ideal sites for adverts thanks to their high-earning user populations.

The leading social networks among Millennials and Gen Z are Instagram and

YouTube, demonstrating the power of bright, eye-popping material that exudes personality.

Women greatly outnumber males on Pinterest, which is acknowledged to have the highest average order value for social shopping.

LinkedIn's user base is well-educated, making it a hotspot for in-depth, industry-specific material that could be more narrow than what you find on Facebook or Twitter.

Don't stretch yourself too thin. Instead, concentrate on networks where your core audience is already engaged.

Do your investigation on your current social media audience

Although the demographic data above offers you insight into each channel, what about your customers? Further investigation has to be done before you can identify what your real-world social clients truly look like.

That's why many organizations employ a social media dashboard that offers an overview of who's following you and how they engage with you on each platform.

4. Establish your most essential measures and KPIs

Your social media approach should be data-driven.

That means concentrating on the social media analytics that count. Rather than concentrating on vanity metrics, dive into data that correlates directly with your aims.

What measurements are we talking about? Check out the breakdown below:

Reach.

Content reach is the number of unique people that viewed your post. How much of your material truly reaches users' feeds?

Clicks.

This is the number of clicks on your content or account. Tracking clicks per campaign are vital to learning what generates interest or pushes consumers to purchase.

Engagement.
This gives information on how well your audience views you and their readiness to connect.

Hashtag performance.
What were your most-used hashtags? Having this answer may help influence the emphasis of your material moving ahead.

Organic and paid likes.
Beyond a basic Like count, these interactions are ascribed to sponsored or organic content. Given how much harder organic interaction is to obtain, many firms resort to advertisements. Knowing these distinctions may help you budget both your ad expenditure and the time you put in various formats.

Sentiment.

This is the measurement of how consumers respond to your content, brand, or hashtag. Did consumers find your latest campaign offensive? What sort of feeling do people connect with your marketing hashtag? It's always preferable to explore deeper and find out how people discuss or feel about your brand.

A successful social media marketing approach is built on data. That said, the figures need to be placed into a framework that matches your original aims.

5. Create (and curate) compelling social material

No surprises here. Your social media marketing approach relies on your content.

At this stage, you should have a very solid sense of what to publish based on your objectives, audience, and brand identity. You presumably feel sure in selecting networks to cover, too.

But what about your content strategy? Below are some ideas and inspiration that might assist.
To assist narrow down the details of what you should be producing and make sure you're generating creative content, here are some social media trends to consider:

- Stories and time-sensitive postings

Stories aren't going away. Tapping into your followers' FOMO (fear of missing out), Stories-style content is both participatory and can't-miss.
Stories are particularly beneficial for bringing your fans behind the scenes and making your social feed seem more personal. For example, imagine how you may utilize Stories to cover an event or take your followers on a trip without them having to leave the safety of the 'gram.

- Short-form video

Fifty-four percent of marketers feel that video is the most beneficial content format for attaining social objectives, and for good reason. Social video is flourishing, particularly with the introduction of TikTok and Instagram Reels. Both long-form and short-form productions continue to dominate the social sphere across all platforms owing to their high interaction rate.

6. Make your social presence as current as possible

Timeliness is probably more crucial than ever for marketers.

Not only are you expected to churn out new information regularly, but also constantly be “on” for your fans.

But you can’t always expect consumers to operate on your clock. Timeliness is a lofty order whether you’re limited on resources or are part of a tiny team.

Let’s look at some ways to optimize your schedule and your time spent on socials.

- Post at the optimal moments to engage

Quick question: when is your brand open to connecting and communicating with customers?

You could find some advised times to publish late in the evening, for example. But if your team isn't there to interact, what's the purpose of publishing at the "preferred" time?

Instead, attempt to ensure your social media or community managers are present and ready to address any product inquiries or complaints when you Tweet or post. Take time to research the optimal times to publish on social media. However, it's just as vital to participating after publishing.

And that takes us to our next point:

Respond to your client inquiries and shout-outs ASAP

Your consumers desire rapid replies. 47% say that good customer service defines a best-in-class company on social media.
Whether it's capitalizing on praise or replying to a query, companies shouldn't leave consumers hanging. According to our research, social is consumers' #1 favorite route for expressing feedback and reaching out with a service problem or concern. But did you know that most people feel businesses should reply to social media posts within four hours?
Designating teams to certain response responsibilities will help your employees function like a well-oiled social media team, whether you're a group of one or 100.

As social algorithms change, organic content has an increasingly challenging time reaching the bulk of your audience. The last thing you want to do is disregard those who do interact and lose out on sending more down your marketing funnel.

7. Assess what's working, and what's not and keep improving

Offline marketing

1) Networking/Face-to-face interactions are still a useful kind of networking and may assist in generating visitors to your website when your new connections are motivated to learn more about you and your company. Being able to put a face to the name may help establish a stronger feeling of brand loyalty among your consumers, so don't ignore the power of a good, old-fashioned handshake. Make your chances for in-person networking by joining local chapters of groups or organizations where your target audience is likely to be located. Over time, this networking may be

reinforced by participation at national conferences for those same associations/organizations.

2) Speaking Engagements

In-person speaking engagements are a wonderful marketing opportunity for a variety of reasons.

Speaking engagements are a terrific approach to creating credibility and promoting thought leadership inside your organization. According to our surveyed Visible Experts, speaking engagements are the second most common method that Visible Experts get leads.

3) Print Publications

While it won't provide you the same SEO advantages as an internet link back to your website, print magazines still have an important purpose in offline marketing. Obtaining relevant placements in industry publications and journals can enhance your brand exposure and highlight your skills. Include print chances as part of your blogger outreach plan and keep a look out for opportunities to appear in both an online and print edition of a magazine.

However, don't seek out print magazines simply for the sake of it. Just like with your online publications, you need to be choosy. Make sure the publications you choose are relevant to your target audience and a reputable source of information.

4) Direct Mail

Even though direct mailers are more expensive than internet marketing, they may still be a powerful lead-generating technique. some members of your target audience may like getting direct mail because it looks more personalized. And the practice of sending direct mail for marketing objectives is far from obsolete. Certain individuals of your target audience may prefer direct mail contact over any other kind of internet communication.

5) Cold Calls

Similarly, cold calls have that personal touch that typically connects with potential customers. Phone conversations are more personal than emails and require a quick response - which may be both good and negative.

Just make sure you have a specific reason for why you're reaching out and be considerate of your phone call recipient's time. Cold calls are also a wonderful method to reach out to prospective marketing partners about a cooperation possibility, like presenting a webinar or generating content together.

6) Print Advertising

Along the same lines as publishing an article in a print newspaper, running print adverts is another strategy for getting in front of more prospective clients. However, it is substantially more difficult to measure the return on investment for print advertising than it is for internet advertisements and they may frequently be more costly to run, so examine your alternatives carefully. Print advertising is ideally positioned in highly targeted magazines where you can assure members of your target audience will see your ad. If feasible, incorporate a URL or a QR code in the print advertising to drive visitors to the landing page, which will help you monitor these campaigns better.

Chapter 4

Retaining your consumers

Customer retention, or client retention, is the act of converting one-time consumers into recurring customers. The term “retention” originates from retaining, and retain is simply a fancy way of saying maintain. So, the purpose of client retention is to maintain your present customers. The aims and techniques of keeping consumers differ by industry: A firm that offers high-end software would have different client retention techniques than an e-commerce shop.

But for all industries, the aim is to give a level of quality and service that keeps customers coming back.

What Are Customer Retention Programs?

Customer retention programs are actions and methods businesses employ to enhance the customer experience.

The purpose of these programs is to encourage consumers to repurchase while also advocating for the brand's product or service. Customer retention programs may take numerous shapes, but we'll confine them to strategies that are geared toward e-commerce company owners like you.

Let's look into some of the customer retention methods that will provide your consumers the motivation, chance, and desire to return to your shop for another transaction.

Why Is Customer Retention Important?

Aside from the fact that it's more costly to recruit new customers than it is to maintain current ones, there are numerous more reasons why customer retention is vital.

Returning customers are 50 percent more likely to buy from you than new clients, and they tend to spend roughly 33 percent more. So not only is it less costly to maintain your consumers, but it's more lucrative in the long term.

Retained consumers might also assist lower your marketing expenditures. Sure, pleased customers are repeat customers, but they also tell their family and friends about you. Word-of-mouth advertising promotes

greater sales than sponsored promotion, up to five times more.
The trust you receive from your delighted consumers will generate more sales, cut your advertising expenditures, and save you money.
You don't want to be that flash-in-the-pan startup. You want true, organic growth that secures future income.

Benefits Of Customer Retention
Here's a brief breakdown of the advantages you'll get from employing retention methods for customers:

- Builds brand recognition and reputation via word-of-mouth advertising from your loyal consumers.
- Gives you the chance to create positive connections with your consumers.

- Allows you to detect and correct issues by obtaining feedback and listening to your customer's demands. Loyal clients are more inclined to test or experiment with your new items. Six times more probable, according to research. Your clients are more ready to be tolerant of errors if they feel devoted to you, which means fewer of those fly-off-the-handle irate consumers.

Calculating Customer Retention Metrics

Before you start establishing a customer retention strategy, you need to identify and comprehend your existing client retention rate. This figure gives you the proportion of consumers who are staying around.

Your client retention rate is simple to determine using the following equation:

(Number of customers at the end of a period – number of consumers gained during that period) / number of customers at the beginning of the period) X 100 = Customer retention rate

Let's break it down.
First, specify the timeframe. The time range is fully up to you. It might be monthly, quarterly, annually, or whatever works best for you and your company.
Keep in mind that when determining the number of customers after the period, you have to consider customer turnover.

For example, You have 3,000 customers at the beginning of the term. You obtained 1,500 new clients over that period but lost 500 due to churn. That implies that after the time you have 4,000 clients.

The equation would look like this:
(4,000 – 1,500) / 3,000) X 100 = 83.3
Customer Retention Rate = 83.3%

Why is this number so important? It tells you how much of your customers are coming back for more. For a benchmark, it's been reported that a 35 percent or higher retention rate in the e-commerce industry means you're doing well.
There are a variety of techniques to conduct client retention marketing. Connecting on social media, email marketing, and establishing realistic expectations, are the top techniques for raising your customer retention rate.

1. Set Realistic Expectations
Setting realistic expectations is very crucial if you're wanting to boost your customer retention rate. It may have a major influence on your business's ability to maintain clients.

Think about factors like shipment times, for example. Most online retailers can't compete with Amazon when it comes to delivery timeframes. But, what you can do instead is work hard to keep your clients updated.

Suppose you have a client who purchases something and then has to wait a few weeks for it to show up. This may go one of two ways:

They have no clue how long delivery will take, and they get progressively more upset every day that their shipment doesn't arrive.

They understood from the outset that it would take a little bit, so the two-week delay is in line with their expectations, so it's no issue at all.

If the aim is to retain consumers, we want to make sure that we're producing this second situation.

And there are tons of ways to achieve that using basic client retention methods.

You may have clear shipping information on your website. You may send emails to customers alerting them that their purchase was received; that their order was processed; and that their item has been delivered.

You may personalize the updates you deliver to your clients with a few clicks in the Shopify backend:

Of course, creating expectations extends much beyond delivery.

Make sure your product descriptions are correct. Make sure there aren't unexpected expenses that show at checkout. Setting clear expectations is a fundamental, but big, step forward and will go a long way when you're seeking to enhance your client retention rates.

2. Create a Loyalty Program

A customer loyalty program should be an intrinsic element of your client retention method. These programs reward your clients by offering them incentives to come back and buy with you.

Once your consumers subscribe to your loyalty program, make them feel special by hooking them up with offers: Give them an early glance at new items, and provide unique offers. This royal treatment will allow your consumers to feel cherished and is the basis of this customer retention approach.

You can even give someone loyalty program benefits before they have opted in. For example, you may send each consumer a discount coupon inside of their purchase confirmation email.

www.ingramcontent.com/pod-product-compliance
Lightning Source LLC
LaVergne TN
LVHW050333160826
845677LV00014B/3608

* 9 7 9 8 3 5 5 9 7 2 0 2 8 *